PACIFIC COAST HORNS
VOLUME 2

TUBA
CENTER STAGE

TUBA

MUSIC MINUS ONE

4708

SUGGESTIONS FOR USING THIS MMO EDITION

We HAVE TRIED to create a product that will provide you an easy way to learn and perform these compositions with a full ensemble in the comfort of your own home. The following MMO features and techniques will help you maximize the effectiveness of the MMO practice and performance system:

Because it involves a fixed accompaniment performance, there is an inherent lack of flexibility in tempo. We have observed generally accepted tempi, and always in the originally intended key, but some may wish to perform at a different tempo, or to slow down or speed up the accompaniment for practice purposes; or to alter the piece to a more comfortable key. For maximum flexibility, you can purchase from MMO specialized CD players & recorders which allow variable speed while maintaining proper pitch, and vice versa. This is an indispensable tool for the serious musician and you may wish to look into purchasing this useful piece of equipment for full enjoyment of all your MMO editions.

We want to provide you with the most useful practice and performance accompaniments possible. If you have any suggestions for improving the MMO system, please feel free to contact us. You can reach us by e-mail at *info@musicminusone.com*.

4708

CONTENTS

ISBN 978-1-59615-792-7
1-59615-792-5

Overture to Clementine

Ken Whitcomb

6

Fascinating Rhythm

Tuba

Words by Ira Gershwin
Music by George Gershwin
arr. Chas Warren

Music Man Medley

Meredith Willson
arr. Chas Warren

Funeral March of a Marionette

Tuba

Charles Gounod
adulterated by Chas Warren

Moderate swing tempo ♩= 76

4 taps - 2 measures

Tuba

A String of Pearls

by Jerry Gray
arr. Chas Warren

MMO 4708

18

Tuba

Bocoxe

Baden Powell
arr. Buttery/Warren

MMO 4708

Minnie the Moocher

Tuba

Words & Music by
Cab Calloway & Irving Mills
arr. Chas Warren

Tuba

Bist du bei mir

(IF THOU BE NEAR)

J. S. Bach
trans. Chas Warren

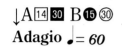

Adagio ♩= 60

3 taps - 1 measure   *sempre legato*

Tuba

Sabre Dance

Aram Khachaturian
arr. Paul Chauvin

MUSIC MINUS ONE
50 Executive Boulevard
Elmsford, New York 10523-1325
1.800.669.7464 (U.S.)/914.592.1188 (International)

www.musicminusone.com
e-mail: info@musicminusone.com